UNTIL WE MEET
Journal

MY GRIEF JOURNAL

This journal belongs to:

If you find this journal contact:

Loss has brought me to this place – the departure of someone dear to me has left an indelible mark on my heart. Through these pages, I hope to find solace in expressing the thoughts and emotions that may be difficult to articulate otherwise. This journal will witness my tears, my laughter as I reminisce, and my attempts to make sense of a reality that feels altered.

Grief is not a linear process; it's a web of emotions that intertwine and challenge our very core. In this journal, I am granting myself permission to embrace the messiness of grief, to explore the highs and lows, and to confront the questions that linger in the depths of my heart.

As I put pen to paper, I acknowledge that this journal is a safe space. It's a place where I can be authentic, where I can wrestle with my feelings, and where I can find the strength to keep moving forward, even when the path feels uncertain.

I am determined to use this journal as a tool for healing. I will reflect on the beautiful moments I shared with _____, the lessons their presence taught me, and the legacy they've left behind. Through my words, I will honour their memory and preserve the impact they had on my life.

There will be days when my entries are filled with tears, and there will be days when I find glimmers of hope amid the sadness. Through it all, I will be kind to myself. I will allow myself to grieve at my own pace, without judgment.

I embark on this journaling journey with an open heart, knowing that while grief is a profound challenge, it can also be a catalyst for growth, empathy, and a deeper understanding of the human experience. I am ready to embrace this journey with all its challenges and revelations, knowing that as I write, I'm taking a step toward healing, with Almighty God as my strength.

_____   _____
Name/signature   Date

"Blessed are those who mourn, for they will be comforted."
When your heart aches with mourning, take comfort in the promise that
God's comforting embrace will soothe your sorrow.
Matthew 5:4

NAME:

KNOWN TO ME AS:

SUNRISE:
BIRTH

SUNSET:
DEATH

Photo/memory/material/item

Photo/memory/material/item

WHO YOU WERE TO ME:

"Cast all your anxiety on him because he cares for you."
As you cast your anxieties onto God, find peace in the
knowledge that He cares for every detail of your life.
1 Peter 5:7

THE FIRST TIME WE MET...

YOUR FAVOURITE....

FOODS, COLOURS, PLACES, SCRIPTURES, ETC...

FUNNIEST MEMORY:

I REMEMBER YOU SAYING...

THINGS I ADMIRED ABOUT YOU:

WHAT I WILL MISS THE MOST...

IF I COULD SPEAK WITH YOU ONE LAST TIME, I WOULD TELL YOU...

AND...

EXPRESS YOUR EMOTIONS:

- Write about how you're feeling.
- Be honest and open about your emotions, whether they are sadness, anger, confusion, or even moments of relief.

"So do not fear, for I am with you; do not be dismayed, for I am your God. I will strengthen you and help you; I will uphold you with my righteous right hand."

Amidst your fears and uncertainties, find courage knowing that God stands beside you, strengthening and guiding you through the darkest valleys.

ISAIAH 41:10 (NIV)

WHEN SOMEONE ASKS: "HOW ARE YOU?"
OPTIONS: "I'M DOING THE BEST I CAN TODAY." "IT'S A HARD DAY." "THANKS FOR ASKING, I'M TAKING THINGS SLOW."

WHEN SOMEONE SAYS: "THEY'RE IN A BETTER PLACE."
YOUR RESPONSE CAN BE: "THAT MAY BE TRUE, BUT I REALLY MISS THEM HERE." "THANKS FOR SAYING THAT."

WHEN SOMEONE AVOIDS MENTIONING THEM AND YOU WANT TO:
SAY: "IT HELPS ME WHEN PEOPLE TALK ABOUT THEM. I LOVE REMEMBERING THEM."

IF IT FEELS OVERWHELMING:
IT'S OKAY TO SAY: "I'D RATHER NOT TALK ABOUT THIS RIGHT NOW, BUT THANK YOU FOR CARING."

USE THESE PAGES AND PHRASES HOWEVER YOU NEED. THERE IS NO WRONG WAY TO GRIEVE, AND NO PRESSURE TO FILL EVERY PAGE. JUST TAKE THE NEXT BREATH, THE NEXT STEP, THE NEXT PAGE—WITH LOVE.

....
....
....

I LOVE OTHERS AS I LOVE MYSELF, FOLLOWING JESUS' COMMAND. (MARK 12:31)

date ....

What happened... where I was when I knew...

I CAN DO ALL THINGS THROUGH CHRIST WHO STRENGTHENS ME. (PHILIPPIANS 4:13)

date

I AM A CHILD OF GOD, CHOSEN AND DEARLY LOVED.
(COLOSSIANS 3:12)

What I wish I could say to you today is...   date _____

_____
_____
_____
_____
_____
_____
_____
_____
_____
_____
_____
_____
_____
_____

Right now, I feel: (tick all that apply)

- [ ] Sad
- [ ] Angry
- [ ] Numb
- [ ] Guilty
- [ ] Confused
- [ ] Relieved
- [ ] Grateful

Why do I think I feel this way today?

_____
_____
_____
_____
_____
_____

THE LORD IS MY STRENGTH AND MY SHIELD; MY HEART TRUSTS IN HIM. (PSALM 28:7)

date

I AM LOVED WITH AN EVERLASTING LOVE

When I began to feel the weight of this loss...   date ....

GOD IS MY REFUGE AND STRENGTH, A PRESENT HELP IN TROUBLE. (PSALM 46:1)

When I began to feel the weight of this loss...   date

MY WORTH IS FOUND IN CHRIST, NOT IN THE OPINIONS OF OTHERS.
(GALATIANS 2:20)

What I wish I could say to you today is...   date ....

IN MY WEAKNESS, GOD'S POWER IS MADE PERFECT. (2 CORINTHIANS 12:9)

date

GOD EQUIPS ME WITH STRENGTH AND MAKES MY WAY PERFECT. (PSALM 18:32)

I miss you most when.... date ....

I AM FEARFULLY AND WONDERFULLY MADE BY GOD. (PSALM 139:14)

date ....

"Praise be to the God... who comforts us in all our troubles."
— 2 Corinthians 1:3–4

Father of mercies, I feel weak and heavy with sorrow. But I thank You that You are the God of all comfort. Wrap me in Your arms, steady me when I stumble, and be my peace when grief overwhelms me. Amen.

GOD'S LOVE FOR ME IS UNCHANGING AND UNCONDITIONAL. (ROMANS 8:38–39)

date _____

I find myself missing...

I TREAT MY BODY AS A TEMPLE OF THE HOLY SPIRIT, HONOURING GOD. (1 CORINTHIANS 6:19-20)

date

I AM CREATED IN GOD'S IMAGE, REFLECTING HIS GLORY. (GENESIS 1:27)

The little everyday things that remind me of you are...   date _____

I FIND MY IDENTITY AND PURPOSE IN CHRIST ALONE. (2 CORINTHIANS 5:17)

date _____

I AM STRONG AND COURAGEOUS, KNOWING THAT
GOD IS WITH ME WHEREVER I GO.

date _____

My thoughts and feeling today are

_____

_____

_____

_____

_____

_____

_____

_____

_____

_____

_____

_____

_____

_____

_____

_____

_____

_____

_____

_____

_____

_____

_____

_____

_____

I AM AN OVERCOMER, EMPOWERED BY GOD TO OVERCOME CHALLENGES AND OBSTACLES.

date ....

"He was despised and rejected... a man of suffering, and familiar with pain." — Isaiah 53:3

Lord Jesus, You know grief. You wept, You mourned, You carried sorrow. Thank You for understanding my broken heart. Be near to me and help me lean on the One who knows what it is to grieve. I pray in Jesus' Name. Amen.

I AM A SERVANT OF GOD, CALLED TO LOVE
AND SERVE OTHERS SELFLESSLY.

A time we laughed together was...   date _____

I HAVE UNWAVERING FAITH IN GOD'S PROMISES AND TRUST IN HIS PERFECT TIMING.

date

I CAST MY ANXIETIES ON GOD, FOR HE CARES FOR ME. (1 PETER 5:7)

date _____

I TRUST IN THE LORD WITH ALL MY HEART AND LEAN NOT ON MY OWN UNDERSTANDING. (PROVERBS 3:5)

REMEMBERING YOUR LOVED ONE:

- Share specific memories or anecdotes about the person you've lost.
- Reflect on the impact they've had on your life and the things you miss about them.

"My flesh and my heart may fail, but God is the strength of my heart and my portion forever."

When you feel weak, be assured that God's strength becomes your own, supporting you even when your heart and body falter.

PSALM 73:26 (NIV)

Something you always used to say was...   date _____

GOD'S PLANS FOR ME ARE GOOD, TO GIVE ME HOPE AND A FUTURE. (JEREMIAH 29:11)

A moment I'll never forget was ...   date

I HAVE PEACE THROUGH CHRIST, WHO HAS
OVERCOME THE WORLD. (JOHN 16:33)

A moment I'll never forget was ...   date

I HAVE FAITH THAT GOD WORKS ALL THINGS TOGETHER FOR MY GOOD. (ROMANS 8:28)

A time we laughed together was..   date ....

I BELIEVE THAT GOD IS ABLE TO DO IMMEASURABLY MORE THAN I ASK OR IMAGINE. (EPHESIANS 3:20)

A moment I'll never forget was ...   date ....

MY FAITH IN JESUS EMPOWERS ME TO LIVE A VICTORIOUS LIFE. (1 JOHN 5:4)

You were my....   date

I CAN DO ALL THINGS THROUGH CHRIST WHO STRENGTHENS ME. (PHILIPPIANS 4:13)

The things you taught me...   date

I AM CONFIDENT THAT GOD'S GRACE IS SUFFICIENT FOR ME. (2 CORINTHIANS 12:9)

Words I would use to describe you... date _____

I TRUST IN GOD'S GUIDANCE AND STEP OUT IN FAITH,
KNOWING HE GOES BEFORE ME. (JOSHUA 1:9)

A moment I'll never forget was ...   date ....

I TRUST IN THE LORD WITH ALL MY HEART AND
ACKNOWLEDGE HIM IN ALL MY WAYS. (PROVERBS 3:6)

date _____

"You have collected all my tears in your bottle. You have recorded each one in your book." — Psalm 56:8

Father, my tears feel endless, but none are wasted. You see each one. Thank You for knowing my pain so deeply. Comfort me with Your presence and remind me that You never turn away from my cries. I know you love me with an everlasting love, continue to hold me in your arms. I need you now. You are my Rock. Amen.

I TRUST IN GOD'S PLAN FOR MY LIFE, KNOWING THAT HE WORKS ALL THINGS TOGETHER FOR MY GOOD.

date ....

A list of things that always made you smile

I SURRENDER MY WORRIES AND ANXIETIES TO GOD, FOR HE CARES FOR ME.

Favourite foods, songs, hobbies   date

I AM FILLED WITH THE PEACE OF CHRIST THAT SURPASSES ALL UNDERSTANDING.

Something you always used to say was...   date _____

I AM EQUIPPED WITH THE ARMOUR OF GOD TO STAND FIRM AGAINST THE SCHEMES OF THE ENEMY.

A time we laughed together was   date ....

I AM A VESSEL OF GOD'S LOVE, SHARING HIS LOVE WITH OTHERS WHEREVER I GO.

date ....

One way I can keep your memory alive is ...

I HAVE A SOUND MIND AND A SPIRIT OF SELF-DISCIPLINE, FOR GOD HAS NOT GIVEN ME A SPIRIT OF FEAR.

A moment I'll never forget was ...   date _____

I AM ROOTED AND GROUNDED IN GOD'S WORD, DRAWING STRENGTH AND WISDOM FROM HIS TRUTH.

date _____

"The Lord is close to the brokenhearted and saves those who are crushed in spirit." — Psalm 34:18

Lord, my heart feels crushed. I don't know how to carry this pain. But You promise to be near the brokenhearted. Draw close to me now. Let me feel the safety of Your nearness. I believe you are with me always. Amen.

MY FAITH IN GOD'S PROMISES GIVES ME HOPE BEYOND CIRCUMSTANCES. (HEBREWS 11:1) date ....

GOD HAS GIVEN ME UNIQUE GIFTS AND TALENTS
FOR HIS PURPOSE. (1 CORINTHIANS 12:7)

date ....

I WALK BY FAITH AND NOT BY SIGHT, KNOWING THAT
GOD'S PROMISES ARE TRUE AND RELIABLE.

COPING STRATEGIES:

- Discuss any coping mechanisms or activities you've tried to manage your grief.
- Explore what worked well and what didn't, and how these activities made you feel.

"He will wipe every tear from their eyes. There will be no more death or mourning or crying or pain, for the old order of things has passed away."

Picture a future where pain and sorrow are no more, and let this hope anchor your heart in times of loss.

REVELATION 21:4 (NIV)

date ....

I AM A LIGHT IN THE WORLD, SHINING GOD'S LOVE
AND TRUTH TO THOSE AROUND ME.

A cause or tradition I want to continue in your honour is...

date _____

I AM A CONQUEROR THROUGH CHRIST JESUS WHO STRENGTHENS ME.

When I feel overwhelmed, I can...　　date _____

I AM GRATEFUL FOR GOD'S ABUNDANT BLESSINGS AND HIS FAITHFULNESS IN EVERY SEASON.

date

A funny moment that still makes me laugh...

I AM A VESSEL OF GOD'S PEACE, BRINGING CALMNESS AND SERENITY TO ANY SITUATION I ENCOUNTER.

date _____

Places we used to go to and memories there.

**I AM A PERSON OF INTEGRITY, LIVING A LIFE
THAT REFLECTS GOD'S CHARACTER AND VALUE.**

One of your quirks I'll never forget...   date

I AM FILLED WITH THE JOY OF THE LORD, WHICH IS MY STRENGTH

If my grief was an image, it would look like this...

date ....

What brings me peace?

....

....

....

....

I AM AN ENCOURAGER, LIFTING OTHERS UP AND SPEAKING LIFE-GIVING WORDS.

Something I never got to ask or say...　　　date _____

I DECLARE THAT I WALK IN THE LIGHT OF CHRIST, AND DARKNESS HAS NO POWER OVER ME (JOHN 8:12).

I wonder what you would say if...

date

I DECLARE THAT GOD FIGHTS FOR ME, AND I NEED ONLY TO BE STILL AND TRUST IN HIS DELIVERANCE

I really need to let go of this regret...　　date _____

I AFFIRM THAT I AM MORE THAN A CONQUEROR THROUGH CHRIST WHO LOVES ME, AND I HAVE VICTORY OVER EVERY ATTACK OF THE ENEMY (ROMANS 8:37).

I need to forgive myself for...   date ....

**I REBUKE EVERY SPIRIT OF HEAVINESS AND DESPAIR,
AND I PUT ON THE GARMENT OF PRAISE**

I notice my grief most when...   date _____

I AM EMPOWERED BY THE HOLY SPIRIT TO WALK IN RIGHTEOUSNESS AND HOLINESS.

date ....

Grief feels like   today...

CHALLENGES AND PROGRESS:

- Write about the challenges you've faced during the grieving process.
- Note any signs of progress or small victories you've experienced.

"God is our refuge and strength, an ever-present help in trouble."

When life's challenges seem insurmountable, find refuge in the fact that God is your steadfast protector and unfailing support.

PSALM 46:1 (NIV)

date _____

When I feel overwhelmed, I can...,

I AFFIRM THAT THE LORD IS MY STRENGTH AND MY SHIELD, AND I TRUST IN HIM TO DELIVER ME FROM EVERY EVIL (PSALM 28:7).

date _____

"The Lord is close to the broken-hearted and saves those who are crushed in spirit." – Psalm 34:18

What would it mean for me to allow comfort in today?

_____
_____
_____
_____
_____
_____
_____
_____
_____
_____
_____
_____
_____
_____
_____
_____
_____
_____

I AFFIRM THAT GOD IS FOR ME, AND IF GOD IS FOR ME, NO ONE CAN STAND AGAINST ME (ROMANS 8:31).

date ....

People I can reach out to:

I HAVE THE HOLY SPIRIT LIVING WITHIN ME, GUIDING AND EMPOWERING ME.

date ....

A memory that brings me comfort in spring:

I AM A VESSEL OF GOD'S LOVE, GRACE, AND TRUTH.

date ....

A memory that brings me comfort in spring:

I AM SURROUNDED BY GOD'S FAVOUR AND BLESSINGS.

date ....

One new thing I want to try this season:

I AM A PEACEMAKER, SPREADING GOD'S LOVE AND RECONCILIATION.

date ....

Ways I can bring joy into the days I feel low

I AM FILLED WITH JOY, PEACE, AND HOPE THROUGH THE HOLY SPIRIT.

Today, I'm feeling... date

I AM A DISCIPLE OF JESUS, COMMITTED TO FOLLOWING HIS TEACHINGS AND EXAMPLE.

A birthday memory I cherish

date

I AM AN INSTRUMENT OF GOD'S HEALING AND RESTORATION.

Long days remind me of…

date

I AM STRONG AND COURAGEOUS, KNOWING THAT
GOD IS WITH ME WHEREVER I GO.

date

"You are the God who sees me." — Genesis 16:13

Father, even when I feel invisible in my grief, You see me. You know my pain, my loneliness, my aching heart. Thank You for being the God who never overlooks me. Help me trust that You see and care. Amen.

I AM FILLED WITH GRATITUDE FOR GOD'S ABUNDANT BLESSINGS IN MY LIFE.

date ....

One way I can honour you this year:

I AFFIRM THAT THE LORD IS MY STRENGTH AND MY SHIELD, AND I TRUST IN HIM TO DELIVER ME FROM EVERY EVIL (PSALM 28:7).

date ....

One way I can reflect or take comfort today:

I AM AN OVERCOMER, EMPOWERED BY GOD TO OVERCOME CHALLENGES AND OBSTACLES.

date _____

One thing I miss about spending this time with you

I AM A SERVANT OF GOD, CALLED TO LOVE AND SERVE OTHERS SELFLESSLY.

date ....

"Come to me, all you who are weary and burdened, and I will give you rest." — Matthew 11:28

Jesus, I am weary from carrying grief. I come to You with my heavy burden. Please give me Your rest. Teach me how to breathe again, and how to let You carry what I cannot. I will bless and praise Your name forever. Although this is such a big change for me, you never change. You are the constant, unchanging, God. You remain the same, today, yesterday and forever. You give me Your peace and I am grateful. Keep me in your arms. I pray in Jesus name. Amen.

I AM CHOSEN, CALLED, AND SET APART FOR A PURPOSE.

SELF-REFLECTION:

- Reflect on how you've changed since the loss.
- Consider how your perspectives, values, or priorities have shifted.

"I consider that our present sufferings are not worth comparing with the glory that will be revealed in us."

Amidst your current sufferings, remember that the glory awaiting you far surpasses any pain you endure now.

ROMANS 8:18 (NIV)

A small way to care for myself today is: date

I HAVE UNWAVERING FAITH IN GOD'S PROMISES AND TRUST IN HIS PERFECT TIMING.

What these days bring up for me...:	date

I AM A VESSEL OF GOD'S GRACE, EXTENDING FORGIVENESS AND COMPASSION TO OTHERS.

A small way to care for myself today is: date _____

I EMBRACE THE POWER OF PRAYER, KNOWING THAT GOD HEARS AND ANSWERS MY PRAYERS.

One thing I miss about spending time with you...

date

I CHOOSE TO DWELL ON THOUGHTS THAT ARE TRUE, NOBLE, RIGHT, PURE, LOVELY, ADMIRABLE, EXCELLENT, AND PRAISEWORTHY.

date ....

Something I can do to protect my heart is...

I RELEASE ALL WORRIES AND ANXIETIES INTO GOD'S HANDS, FOR HE IS MY REFUGE AND STRENGTH.

A birthday memory I cherish...   date

I TRUST IN THE LORD'S GUIDANCE AND DIRECTION, KNOWING THAT HE WILL LEAD ME ON THE PATH OF TRIUMPH OVER OBSTACLES.

date _____

The long summer days remind me of...

I AM GUIDED BY THE HOLY SPIRIT, WHO LEADS ME IN PATHS OF RIGHTEOUSNESS AND WISDOM.

date _____

What feels like it is starting to heal?

I AM AN OVERCOMER, BECAUSE CHRIST HAS ALREADY OVERCOME THE WORLD.

date _____

What feels like it is just starting to heal?:

I FIND STRENGTH IN YOUR PRESENCE, KNOWING THAT YOU ARE WITH ME ALWAYS.

date ....

Today I'm feeling....

I AM A SOURCE OF ENCOURAGEMENT AND INSPIRATION TO THOSE AROUND ME.

date ....

A small way to care for myself today is:

I WALK IN HUMILITY, RECOGNISING THAT GOD'S POWER IS MADE PERFECT IN MY WEAKNESS.

date _____

The holidays are the hardest because...

"My Father... is greater than all; no one can snatch them out of my Father's hand." — John 10:29

Lord, I take comfort knowing my loved one is safe in Your hands. Thank You that no power can take them from You. When I miss them deeply, remind me they are secure with You. Amen.

I TRUST IN GOD'S UNFAILING LOVE AND BELIEVE THAT HE WORKS ALL THINGS FOR MY GOOD.

date ....

Special days... what these days bring up for me...

I CHOOSE TO REJOICE IN THE LORD ALWAYS, FINDING JOY IN HIS PRESENCE AND FAITHFULNESS.

date ....

One way I can reflect and take comfort today...

I EMBRACE A MINDSET OF ABUNDANCE, KNOWING THAT GOD'S BLESSINGS OVERFLOW IN MY LIFE.

date ....

A small way to care for myself today is:

I AM A VESSEL OF PEACE, SPREADING HARMONY AND RECONCILIATION WHEREVER I GO.

date ....

I AM A CONQUEROR OVER TRIBULATIONS: "I HAVE TOLD YOU THESE THINGS, SO THAT IN ME YOU MAY HAVE PEACE. IN THIS WORLD YOU WILL HAVE TROUBLE. BUT TAKE HEART! I HAVE OVERCOME THE WORLD" (JOHN 16:33).

date _____

"He heals the broken-hearted and binds up their wounds." — Psalm 147:3

Lord, my heart feels shattered, but You promise healing. Please bind up the broken pieces of my soul. Day by day, heal me and help me believe that joy can come again. Amen.

I HAVE THE COURAGE TO FACE CHALLENGES HEAD-ON, KNOWING THAT GOD IS WITH ME EVERY STEP OF THE WAY.

SUPPORT SYSTEM:

- Acknowledge whoever has been supporting you through your grief journey.
- Express gratitude for their presence and understanding.

"Praise be to the God and Father of our Lord Jesus Christ, the Father of compassion and the God of all comfort, who comforts us in all our troubles, so that we can comfort those in any trouble with the comfort we ourselves receive from God."

As you receive God's comfort in your grief, remember that your experiences can transform into a source of comfort for others in their times of trouble.

2 CORINTHIANS 1:3-4 (NIV)

date ....

The people who have shown me kindness ...

**I EMBRACE DIVINE OPPORTUNITIES AND STEP OUT IN FAITH,
KNOWING THAT GOD GOES BEFORE ME.**

date _____

"My grace is sufficient for you, for my power is made perfect in weakness." — 2 Corinthians 12:9

Father, I feel weak and helpless. But You say Your grace is enough. Please be my strength today. Help me not to fear my weakness, but to find comfort in Your power working in me.

"PEACE I LEAVE WITH YOU; MY PEACE I GIVE YOU. I DO NOT GIVE TO YOU AS THE WORLD GIVES. DO NOT LET YOUR HEARTS BE TROUBLED AND DO NOT BE AFRAID"
(JOHN 14:27).

date _____

GOD DOES NOT GIVE US A SPIRIT OF FEAR BUT OF POWER,
LOVE, AND A SOUND MIND (2 TIMOTHY 1:7).

date _____

"Weeping may endure for a night, but joy comes in the morning." — Psalm 30:5

Lord, my nights feel long with tears. But You promise that joy will come. Help me trust that brighter days are ahead, even if I cannot see them yet. Hold me until that morning comes. I pray believing. In Jesus Name I pray. Amen.

I AM STRONG IN THE LORD, AND HIS POWER ENABLES ME TO OVERCOME ANY OBSTACLE THAT COMES MY WAY.

date ....

A message I could send to someone who is grieving today...

I AM NOT DEFINED BY MY CIRCUMSTANCES, BUT BY MY UNWAVERING FAITH AND TRUST IN GOD'S FAITHFULNESS.

date _____

"Never will I leave you; never will I forsake you." — Hebrews 13:5

Father, I feel so alone. But You promise never to leave me. Remind me of Your presence when I feel abandoned. Let me sense Your nearness in the quiet and the stillness. Amen.

I AM EMPOWERED BY THE HOLY SPIRIT, WHO EQUIPS ME WITH THE STRENGTH AND WISDOM TO NAVIGATE DIFFICULT SITUATIONS.

date _____

I'm grateful for....

THROUGH CHRIST, I AM MORE THAN A CONQUEROR, AND I CAN OVERCOME ANY OBSTACLE THAT STANDS IN MY PATH.

date _____

> "The peace of God, which transcends all understanding, will guard your hearts and minds." — Philippians 4:7

Lord, grief makes my mind restless and my heart heavy. Please guard my heart with Your peace. Even when I cannot understand, let Your Spirit calm me with a peace the world cannot give. Amen.

I AM RESILIENT IN THE FACE OF ADVERSITY, KNOWING THAT GOD'S GRACE IS SUFFICIENT FOR ME.

date

I CHOOSE TO FOCUS ON GOD'S PROMISES RATHER THAN THE OBSTACLES BEFORE ME, KNOWING THAT HE IS FAITHFUL TO FULFIL HIS WORD.

date _____

"God is our refuge and strength, an ever-present help in trouble." — Psalm 46:1

Father, I feel shaken by loss. Be my rock when the ground beneath me feels unsteady. Shelter me in Your refuge and remind me I am not without hope. Amen.

I AM NOT ALONE IN MY STRUGGLES, FOR GOD WALKS BESIDE ME AND CARRIES ME THROUGH THE CHALLENGES I FACE.

date _____

"Even though I walk through the valley of the shadow of death, I will fear no evil, for you are with me." – Psalm 23:4

What does it mean for me to not walk alone through grief?

_____
_____
_____
_____
_____
_____
_____
_____
_____
_____
_____

I AM AN OVERCOMER BECAUSE CHRIST HAS OVERCOME THE WORLD, AND HIS VICTORY RESIDES WITHIN ME.

date

I HAVE THE STRENGTH TO PERSEVERE AND PRESS ON, EVEN WHEN CIRCUMSTANCES SEEM OVERWHELMING.

date ....

"Even the very hairs of your head are all numbered." — Matthew 10:30

Lord, You know me so completely. You know the depths of my grief, the loneliness I hide from others. Thank You that I am fully known by You, and fully loved. Amen.

I AM CONFIDENT IN MY ABILITY TO OVERCOME OBSTACLES BECAUSE I AM ROOTED IN GOD'S LOVE AND HIS UNFAILING PROMISES.

LESSONS AND INSIGHTS:

- Share any insights or lessons you've gained from your grief experience.
- Write about your personal growth and new perspectives on life.

"The Lord is my rock, my fortress and my deliverer; my God is my rock, in whom I take refuge, my shield and the horn of my salvation, my stronghold."

Lean on God, your unshakeable fortress, who shields you from life's storms and provides unwavering strength.

PSALM 18:2 (NIV)

A way I surprised myself recently...   date _____

I AM FILLED WITH COURAGE AND BOLDNESS, KNOWING THAT GOD HAS GIVEN ME A SPIRIT OF POWER, LOVE, AND A SOUND MIND.

date _____

Where am I still healing??

I HAVE THE POWER TO DEMOLISH STRONGHOLDS AND CAST DOWN EVERY THOUGHT THAT EXALTS ITSELF AGAINST THE KNOWLEDGE OF GOD.

date ....

I'm really proud of myself for...

....
....
....
....
....
....
....
....
....
....
....
....
....
....
....
....
....
....
....
....
....
....
....
....

I AM ROOTED AND GROUNDED IN GOD'S LOVE, AND HIS LOVE CASTS OUT ALL FEAR AND DOUBT SOWN BY THE ENEMY.

date _____

How have I experienced comfort in unexpected ways...

I AM AN OVERCOMER BY THE BLOOD OF THE LAMB AND THE WORD OF MY TESTIMONY, AND I WILL NOT BE SHAKEN OR DEFEATED BY THE ENEMY'S SCHEMES.

Things that bring me peace..   date _____

_____
_____
_____
_____
_____
_____
_____
_____
_____
_____
_____
_____
_____
_____
_____
_____
_____
_____
_____
_____
_____
_____
_____

I AM NOT DISCOURAGED BY SETBACKS OR CHALLENGES, FOR I KNOW THAT GOD IS WORKING ALL THINGS TOGETHER FOR MY ULTIMATE VICTORY.

date ....

A small thing that made me smile today was...

I AM FILLED WITH HOPE AND OPTIMISM, FOR I KNOW THAT GOD'S PLANS FOR ME ARE PLANS FOR A FUTURE FILLED WITH HOPE AND SUCCESS.

date ....

Today, I'm proud of myself for...

I AM FILLED WITH HOPE AND OPTIMISM, FOR I KNOW THAT GOD'S PLANS FOR ME ARE PLANS FOR A FUTURE FILLED WITH HOPE AND SUCCESS.

date ....

Today I am grateful for...

I AM AN OVERCOMER IN CHRIST JESUS, AND I EMBRACE THE CHALLENGES BEFORE ME AS OPPORTUNITIES FOR GOD TO DEMONSTRATE HIS POWER AND FAITHFULNESS.

date ....

Even in loss, I see beauty in...

I DECLARE THAT THE LIGHT OF GOD SHINES BRIGHTLY IN ME, DISPELLING ALL DARKNESS AND CONFUSION.

date ....

Today I allowed myself to enjoy....

I AFFIRM THAT I AM A CHILD OF GOD, AND HIS LOVE SURROUNDS AND PROTECTS ME AT ALL TIMES.

date ....

A small way to care for myself today is:

I AFFIRM THAT THE PLANS OF THE ENEMY ARE RENDERED POWERLESS IN THE PRESENCE OF GOD'S TRUTH AND RIGHTEOUSNESS.

I'm proud of myself for....   date _____

I DECLARE THAT GOD'S PEACE GUARDS MY HEART AND MIND, AND I AM NOT SWAYED BY FEAR OR ANXIETY.

date ....

Today, one things that made me smile was...

I AFFIRM THAT I AM ANOINTED BY GOD TO WALK IN VICTORY, AND NO WEAPON FORMED AGAINST ME SHALL PROSPER.

UNANSWERED QUESTIONS:

- Write down any lingering questions or unresolved feelings you have about your loss.
- You don't have to have all the answers; this is a space to acknowledge your feelings.

"He heals the brokenhearted and binds up their wounds."

In times of brokenness, remember that the Lord draws near to you, offering solace and healing for your wounded heart.

PSALM 34:18 (NIV)

I'm still asking myself...   date _____

I HAVE THE HOLY SPIRIT LIVING WITHIN ME, GUIDING AND EMPOWERING ME.

date _____

"I thank my God every time I remember you." — Philippians 1:3

Father, thank You for the gift of memories. Though they bring tears, they also bring joy. Help me to cherish the laughter, the love, and the moments we shared, and let those memories bring comfort. Amen.

I AM CHOSEN, CALLED, AND SET APART FOR A PURPOSE.

date ....

I AM A VESSEL OF GOD'S LOVE, GRACE, AND TRUTH.

date

"Those who hope in the Lord will renew their strength."
— Isaiah 40:31

Lord, my strength feels gone. But my hope is in You. Please renew me each day. Lift me up when I grow weary and help me walk this road of grief with hope. Amen.

I AM SURROUNDED BY GOD'S FAVOUR AND BLESSINGS.

date

I AM A PEACEMAKER, SPREADING GOD'S LOVE AND RECONCILIATION.

date

I AM FILLED WITH JOY, PEACE, AND HOPE THROUGH THE HOLY SPIRIT.

date

I AM A DISCIPLE OF JESUS, COMMITTED TO FOLLOWING HIS TEACHINGS AND EXAMPLE

date

I AM AN INSTRUMENT OF GOD'S HEALING AND RESTORATION.

date _____

I AM FILLED WITH GRATITUDE FOR GOD'S ABUNDANT BLESSINGS IN MY LIFE

date _____

"He will wipe every tear from their eyes. There will be no more death or mourning or crying or pain." — Revelation 21:4

Father, I long for the day when You will wipe away every tear. Until then, hold me close. Give me courage to face today, and hope to look forward to the day of no more sorrow. Amen.

I AM STRONG AND COURAGEOUS, KNOWING THAT GOD IS WITH ME WHEREVER I GO.

date _____

I DECLARE THAT GOD'S ANGELS ENCAMP AROUND ME, SHIELDING ME FROM EVERY SCHEME OF THE ENEMY.

date ....

I AFFIRM THAT GOD'S FAVOUR RESTS UPON ME, AND HE GOES BEFORE ME TO MAKE A WAY WHERE THERE SEEMS TO BE NO WAY.

date

I DECLARE THAT GOD'S PLANS FOR ME ARE GOOD, AND HE WORKS ALL THINGS TOGETHER FOR MY ULTIMATE GOOD.

LOOKING AHEAD:

- Consider your hopes and fears for the future without your loved one.
- Reflect on how you see your life moving forward. Explain what you will do to find strength.

"He heals the brokenhearted and binds up their wounds."

Just as a loving physician binds wounds, God heals your broken heart with His tender care and limitless compassion.

PSALM 147:3 (NIV)

date ....

What this new normal looks like now...

I DECLARE THAT I AM MORE THAN A CONQUEROR THROUGH CHRIST WHO LOVES ME,
AND I AM EQUIPPED TO OVERCOME ANY SPIRITUAL BATTLE.

date

I give myself permission to...

GOD EQUIPS ME WITH STRENGTH AND MAKES MY WAY PERFECT. (PSALM 18:32)

date ....

I give myself permission to....

I AM FEARFULLY AND WONDERFULLY MADE BY GOD. (PSALM 139:14)

date ....

On their birthday, I will...

I DECLARE THAT THE LIGHT OF GOD SHINES BRIGHTLY IN ME, DISPELLING ALL DARKNESS AND CONFUSION.

date _____

> "You keep track of all my sorrows... You have collected all my tears in your bottle."
> — Psalm 56:8

Father, my tears seemed endless. Yet I know none of them are wasted, for You see every one. Thank You for knowing my heart so deeply and for holding my grief. Help me to rest in the truth that You are with me in my pain. I know time heals. I have hope in you. I am blessed to have the opportunity to live, breathe, fulfill my purpose and make you proud of me. Tell me your plans for my life and I will be obedient to you. I will use my growth to make a difference in the lives of others, while remembering the best memories about the one who rests with you now. Amen

GOD'S LOVE FOR ME IS UNCHANGING AND UNCONDITIONAL. (ROMANS 8:38-39))

During holidays, I might...   date

I LOVE OTHERS AS I LOVE MYSELF, FOLLOWING JESUS' COMMAND. (MARK 12:31)

date ....

Ways I can include the memories in everyday life...

I TREAT MY BODY AS A TEMPLE OF THE HOLY SPIRIT, HONOURING GOD. (1 CORINTHIANS 6:19-20)

date ....

Routines and habits that have stayed the same...

I AM FILLED WITH HOPE AND OPTIMISM, FOR I KNOW THAT GOD'S PLANS FOR ME ARE PLANS FOR A FUTURE FILLED WITH HOPE AND SUCCESS.

In the future, I would love to...

date _____

I AM A CHILD OF GOD, CHOSEN AND DEARLY LOVED. (COLOSSIANS 3:12)

date ....

A memory that makes me laugh out loud

MY WORTH IS FOUND IN CHRIST, NOT IN THE OPINIONS OF OTHERS. (GALATIANS 2:20)

A way I surprised myself recently...   date _____

I CHOOSE TO DWELL ON THOUGHTS THAT ARE TRUE, NOBLE, RIGHT, PURE, LOVELY, ADMIRABLE, EXCELLENT, AND PRAISEWORTHY.

A small way to care for myself today is: date _____

I AM CREATED IN GOD'S IMAGE, REFLECTING HIS GLORY. (GENESIS 1:27)

date _____

One of our inside jokes was...

_____

I FIND MY IDENTITY AND PURPOSE IN CHRIST ALONE.
(2 CORINTHIANS 5:17)

My hopes for the future...

date

GOD IS MY REFUGE AND STRENGTH, A PRESENT HELP IN TROUBLE. (PSALM 46:1)

date ....

I EMBRACE THE POWER OF PRAYER, KNOWING THAT
GOD HEARS AND ANSWERS MY PRAYERS.

date ....

I RELEASE ALL WORRIES AND ANXIETIES INTO GOD'S HANDS,
FOR HE IS MY REFUGE AND STRENGTH.

date _____

I AM AN OVERCOMER IN CHRIST JESUS, AND I EMBRACE THE CHALLENGES BEFORE ME AS OPPORTUNITIES FOR GOD TO DEMONSTRATE HIS POWER AND FAITHFULNESS.

CLOSING THOUGHTS:

- Summarise your goodbye by revisiting the main emotions, thoughts, or themes you discussed. And how you plan to honour their legacy.
- End with a positive or hopeful note, even if it's a short one.

"Blessed are those who mourn,
for they will be comforted."

When your heart aches with mourning, take comfort in the promise that God's comforting embrace will soothe your sorrow.

MATTHEW 5:4

date ……………………………………

What I have learned about myself through this…

I CAN DO ALL THINGS THROUGH CHRIST WHO STRENGTHENS ME. (PHILIPPIANS 4:13)

date _____

I AM FILLED WITH COURAGE AND BOLDNESS, KNOWING THAT GOD HAS GIVEN ME A SPIRIT OF POWER, LOVE, AND A SOUND MIND.

What message would I share with someone else just starting their grief journey?   date _____

I AM CONFIDENT IN MY ABILITY TO OVERCOME OBSTACLES BECAUSE I AM ROOTED IN GOD'S LOVE AND HIS UNFAILING PROMISES.

date ....

I BELIEVE THAT GOD IS ABLE TO DO IMMEASURABLY MORE
THAN I ASK OR IMAGINE. (EPHESIANS 3:20)

date

I HAVE THE POWER TO DEMOLISH STRONGHOLDS AND CAST DOWN EVERY THOUGHT THAT EXALTS ITSELF AGAINST THE KNOWLEDGE OF GOD.

date

MY FAITH IN JESUS EMPOWERS ME TO LIVE A VICTORIOUS LIFE. (1 JOHN 5:4)

date _____

I AM ROOTED AND GROUNDED IN GOD'S LOVE, AND HIS LOVE CASTS OUT ALL FEAR AND DOUBT SOWN BY THE ENEMY.

date

I AFFIRM THAT I AM MORE THAN A CONQUEROR THROUGH CHRIST WHO LOVES ME, AND I HAVE VICTORY OVER EVERY ATTACK OF THE ENEMY (ROMANS 8:37).

date

I REBUKE EVERY SPIRIT OF HEAVINESS AND DESPAIR, AND I PUT ON THE GARMENT OF PRAISE.

date

I AM EMPOWERED BY THE HOLY SPIRIT TO
WALK IN RIGHTEOUSNESS AND HOLINESS.

date ....

GOD GIVES ME BEAUTY FOR ASHES AND JOY INSTEAD OF MOURNING

date

I TRUST IN THE LORD WITH ALL MY HEART AND LEAN NOT ON MY OWN UNDERSTANDING. (PROVERBS 3:5)

date _____

I AM A CONQUEROR OVER TRIBULATIONS: "I HAVE TOLD YOU THESE THINGS, SO THAT IN ME YOU MAY HAVE PEACE. IN THIS WORLD YOU WILL HAVE TROUBLE. BUT TAKE HEART! I HAVE OVERCOME THE WORLD" (JOHN 16:33).

Where do you go from here?

Your journal provides a way to support psychological closure from your loss. However, you may want to revisit your thoughts and memories as you heal.

The following pages can be used to record the date you revisited your Until We Meet journal and your thoughts and reflections at the time.

"You turned my wailing into dancing; you removed my sackcloth and clothed me with joy, that my heart may sing your praises and not be silent. Lord my God, I will praise you forever."

PSALM 30:11-12 (NIV)

Our faith reminds us that to be absent in body is to be present with the Lord. We have a hope for the future. Just as God turned sorrow into dancing in this scripture verse, trust that He will replace your mourning with joyous songs that celebrate His goodness.

I AM FILLED WITH HOPE AND OPTIMISM, FOR I KNOW THAT GOD'S PLANS FOR ME ARE PLANS FOR A FUTURE FILLED WITH HOPE AND SUCCESS.

I AM FILLED WITH GOD'S PEACE THAT SURPASSES ALL UNDERSTANDING, AND IT GUARDS MY HEART AND MIND FROM THE ATTACKS OF THE ENEMY.

I AM CONFIDENT IN MY ABILITY TO OVERCOME OBSTACLES BECAUSE I AM ROOTED IN GOD'S LOVE AND HIS UNFAILING PROMISES.

I DECLARE THAT I AM FILLED WITH THE HOLY SPIRIT, AND HIS POWER ENABLES ME TO OVERCOME ANY OBSTACLE.

"BUT THE WISDOM THAT COMES FROM HEAVEN IS FIRST OF ALL PURE; THEN PEACE-LOVING, CONSIDERATE, SUBMISSIVE, FULL OF MERCY AND GOOD FRUIT, IMPARTIAL AND SINCERE" (JAMES 3:17).

"EACH ONE SHOULD TEST THEIR OWN ACTIONS. THEN THEY CAN TAKE PRIDE IN THEMSELVES ALONE, WITHOUT COMPARING THEMSELVES TO SOMEONE ELSE, FOR EACH ONE SHOULD CARRY THEIR OWN LOAD." GALATIANS 6:4-5,

I DECLARE THAT I AM HIDDEN IN THE SHELTER OF THE MOST HIGH, AND
NO EVIL CAN COME NEAR ME (PSALM 91:1).

Memories that make me smile

Attach any memorabilia, photos, cinema ticket, wrapper of their favourite sweet...

Check out our other journals:

 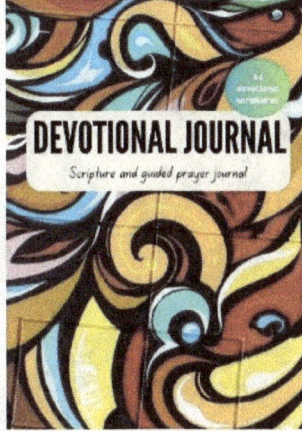 
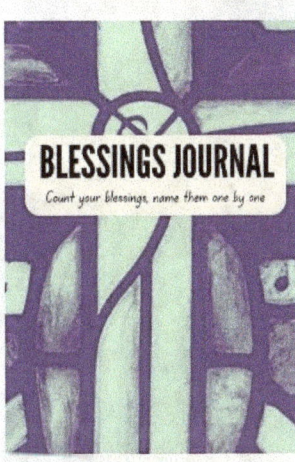  
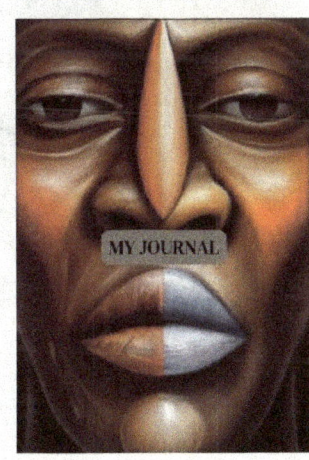 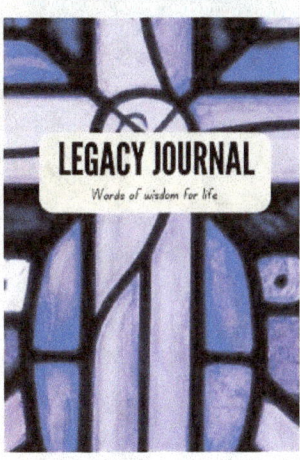 

YOUR JOURNAL, YOUR JOURNEY,
YOUR SPIRITUAL GROWTH

W W W . G I D D Y M O O S E . C O M